CW00369761

THE ILLUSTRATED
ELVIS PRESLEY

THE ILLUSTRATED
ELVIS PRESLEY

GEOFFREY GIULIANO
BRENDA GIULIANO
and
DEBORAH LYNN BLACK

SUNBURST BOOKS

DEDICATION

To Leif Leavesley for overcoming the odds and finding his future. And to Avalon and India for bringing so much joy into our lives.

GG & BG

Text and illustration copyright © Indigo Editions Ltd. 1994
Design copyright © Sunburst Books 1994

This edition published 1994 by Sunburst Books,
Deacon House, 65 Old Church Street, London SW3 5BS.

All rights reserved. No part of this publication may be reproduced, stored in a retrieval system, or transmitted in any form or by any means, electronic, mechanical, photocopying, recording or otherwise, without the prior permission of the publisher.

Every effort has been made to trace the ownership of all copyrighted material and to secure permission from copyright holders. In the event of any question arising as to the use of any material, we will be pleased to make the necessary corrections in future editions.

ISBN 1 85778 036 1

Printed and bound in China

CONTENTS

CHAPTER ONE

OUT OF NOWHERE

"I always felt lonely, maybe even incomplete when I was little. I suppose it might have been different if my brother had lived. A lot of things might have been different. But he didn't and I grew up alone. I've learned to live with the loneliness."

Elvis Presley

Above: Elvis Presley, perhaps the greatest rock'n'roller of all time.

Opposite: The famous Presley profile.

ELVIS ARON Presley ** was born to sharecroppers, Vernon and the former Gladys Love Smith, at 4.35 am on the windy, snowy night of 8th January, 1935 in East Tupelo, Mississippi. However, the brief joy that followed the traumatic labor was shattered when, just thirty-five minutes later, Gladys delivered a second son, Elvis' stillborn twin, Jesse Garon. It was a tragedy that would shape the future of Tupelo's most famous son.

Tupelo's east side slums were a long way from the comfortable and privileged life the future king of rock'n'roll would eventually come to know. The Presleys' meager two-room, thirty by fifteen foot shack was clear evidence of the impoverished conditions of a family only a hair's breadth from utter poverty. Vernon Presley, unable to find farm work in the Great American Depression, drifted from one dead-end job to another; milkman, paint can packer and truck driver. When Elvis was still a youngster, a desperate Vernon forged a lumber company check for $100 and, as a result, served nine months in Mississippi's tough Parchman Penitentiary.

While her husband was away, Gladys was forced to move in with relatives, taking in work as a seamstress and laundress. Her weekly walks to the welfare office with Elvis in tow attracted disparaging stares and hushed comments of "white trash".

*[** Author's note: Although on Presley's birth certificate his middle name appeared as Aron, this was a mistake on the part of his father. Throughout his life he used the conventional spelling, Aaron, and this is how the name appears on his gravestone.]*

To his neighbors, Elvis was known as a "sad-eyed, tow-headed, skinny fellow, real quiet and shy." In fact, he was so unremarkable, nearly invisible, that not a single schoolmate remembers him from his elementary school days.

What he lacked in material wealth though, Gladys more than made up for in manners. "I had to be polite and do the right things," Elvis later remembered. "My folks were real strict. I rebelled sometimes, but I guess their strictness was the best thing that ever happened to me. My Mom and Dad loved me too much to ever spoil me, even though I was an only child."

Unfortunately Gladys reacted to the loss of Jesse by overprotecting her only son. Elvis was seldom allowed to play outside, locked up instead in his uncle's house, a veritable prisoner, according to his aunt Lillian. "A boy needs air, girl," she told her sister. "He thinks he's bein' punished and he ain't doin' nothin'."

Elvis recalled: "I couldn't even go down to the creek with the other kids and swim. That's why I'm no swimmer today." Instead he spent lonely days throwing fists of clay at tin cans, developing a bullseye aim that would serve him well in his army days.

When he started kindergarten, Gladys would walk Elvis to school, a practice she continued daily into high school. She even insisted he take his own cutlery so that he wouldn't pick up germs from his classmates.

Gladys' obsession with her dead son made a deep impression on Elvis. Jesse was the constant, invisible presence, the wonder boy who would have grown up to be an achiever. His mother continuously urged Elvis to pray to Jesse and ask him for guidance. "He's our guardian angel in Heaven," she would tell him. "For as long as I can remember I've been talking to Jesse," Presley would later confess. His belief that half of his soul died at birth prevented him from enjoying his later success to the full. "If only Jesse were here," he lamented frequently throughout his life.

Presley's love of music manifested itself at an early age and was rooted in the gospel singing at the local Assembly of God church, better known as the Holy Rollers. "I remember taking Elvis to church," related Gladys, "and even when he was an infant he'd squirm in my lap whenever the singin' would start. He tried singin' before he could even talk."

One of Gladys' favorite memories was of a three-year-old Elvis leaping from her lap to go racing down the aisle singing and dancing to the hymns. "He was born with a gift for music. He had a knack for it, the voice of an angel."

He learned not only to sing, but also to perform. Many years later a reporter asked Presley where he picked up his revolutionary stage gyrations. "We used to go to these religious singings all the time," he said. "There were these perfectly fine singers, but nobody responded to them. Then there was the preachers and they cut up all over the place, jumpin' on the piano, movin' every which way. The audience loved them. I guess I learned from them."

Presley's close friend, Earl Greenwood, recalled: "His singing voice was high, but incredibly clear. Out of the corner of my eyes I saw tears in Gladys' eyes."

Opposite: Gathering around the piano for a good, old fashioned gospel session.
Left to right: Vernon, Gladys and Elvis Presley.

Presley in Las Vegas, circa 1956.

Opposite, main picture: Elvis at the height of his astounding career.

Opposite, inset: Presley and his cousin, Gene Smith, with their dates for the Home High School prom.

The Presleys formed a vocalist trio in church, as well as at camp and revival meetings. A neighbor commented, "You just never heard anyone sing hymns like those three. It would just about curl your hair."

Added Elvis, "Maybe I wasn't always in tune, but you could sure hear me above the rest!"

Presley's first public appearance came at the age of ten, when his school principal, impressed with his voice, entered him in a contest at the 1945 Mississippi-Alabama Fair and Dairy Show. Standing on a chair to reach the microphone, Elvis sang, unaccompanied, a sentimental ballad called *Old Shep*, about a boy and his dog.

"Elvis just walked himself up to that little ol' platform, his legs quiverin' a bit and sang without any music at all," recalled a proud Vernon. "In a real powerful voice too. Darn if he didn't sing better than that fellow with the guitar."

Presley's strong performance won him second prize, $5 and free rides all day. He would later record the song for his second album, *Elvis*.

The following January for his eleventh birthday Elvis got his hands on his first guitar. Ironically, despite his love of music, it was a .22 caliber shotgun that the boy had his heart set on. However, when Gladys took him down to the Tupelo Hardware Store, she had distinctly different ideas.

"You don't want no shotgun. I saved all this time to get you a guitar, for you to use singin'. If you get good enough maybe the minister'll let you play in church."

Of the three models, Gladys paid $7.75 to buy him the most expensive. Thoughts of a rifle promptly vanished, as young Elvis delighted in his birthday gift. An uncle showed him a few rudimentary chords, but Elvis was largely self-taught, simply by listening to the radio and copying the lusty Mississippi Delta blues he heard every night.

"I dug real lowdown Mississippi singers, mostly Big Bill Broonzy, Big Boy Crudup," he revealed. "I got scolded at home for listening to them, sinful music, they said it was. Which never bothered me, I guess."

Cousin Hershell Presley recalls, "I remember Elvis used to carry that old guitar around. He loved that guitar. It didn't have but three strings on it most of the time, but he could sure beat the dickens out of it."

Meanwhile, all was not well at home. The pressures of being a working mother, coupled with Vernon's imprisonment and a lifelong struggle with poverty took its toll on Gladys and she began drinking to the point of missing work. Eventually she developed a chronic cough and swollen ankles, which made walking painful. Still only in her thirties, she looked twice her age, with dark hollows beneath deeply bloodshot eyes and red blotchy skin. In a small town like Tupelo, a lady boozer was a cause for scandal. Gladys was the talk of the neighborhood, despite consum-

Opposite: Presley at the beginning of his career, attacking a melody in the mid fifties.

ing large quantities of onion to disguise the smell of the liquor on her breath. At home the topic was never discussed, and as far as Elvis knew, Mama simply had another one of her 'migraines'.

In 1948 Vernon Presley was released from jail and found himself without work and flat broke. On the spur of the moment one September day he announced that they were moving. Remembers Elvis: "We left Tupelo overnight. Dad packed all of our belongings and put them in the trunk of a 1939 Plymouth. We just headed to Memphis. Things had to be better."

But life at 572 Poplar Avenue in the bustling Tennessee metropolis, if anything, was far worse. The Presley family moved into a one-room apartment without even a kitchen or sink and had to share a bathroom with five other families.

On top of these deplorable conditions at home, Elvis experienced a profound culture shock, as he found himself one of 1600 students at Humes High, twice the entire population of East Tupelo. Painfully self-conscious and shy, the proverbial country hick in overalls was lost in the big city. Predictably, Elvis withdrew into himself.

Determined to find a way to distinguish himself, however, Presley soon underwent a drastic change. He created his new look from a combination of two factors: one was his love of the comic book hero, Captain Marvel Junior, whose glossy black hair and mission to save the world captured Elvis' active imagination. Presley would later adopt Marvel's lightning bolt insignia as part of his renowned TCB (Taking Care of Business) logo.

The other half of his image was picked up during his frequent visits to the local movie-house, where he was much taken by a character played by Tony Curtis, the alienated, sensitive, misunderstood anti-hero in *City Across the River*. After much experimenting with hair style and clothing, Elvis launched his junior year in a loud pink shirt, white buck shoes, sideburns and his dark blonde hair dyed black and in a greasy ducktail.

Earl Greenwood, in Memphis on a visit, was shocked by the boy's appearance. "I stopped dead in my tracks when I saw him. His blonde hair was gone, replaced by long, jet black, lacquered locks. He could have hit a truck head on and survived!"

Explained Presley: "I was a nobody, a small town kid in a big city, not too good in my classes and kinda shy. All the other guys wore GI haircuts and I wanted to look older, be different. Mostly I wanted to be noticed. But it got pretty weird. They used to see me coming down the street and say 'Hot dang, let's get him, he's a squirrel, he just came down outta the trees!'"

Childhood friend, Red West, who went on to become a Presley bodyguard, remembers constant hassles: "He went out for football but lasted only a few weeks because he refused to cut his hair. One time he was pinned to the wall by a group of rowdy teammates about to give him a haircut by force. He was looking like a frightened little animal and I just couldn't stand seeing it. I helped him escape, but to this day I can still see that face of Elvis', a child's face asking for help."

Presley might have forever languished in high school obscurity if it had not been for his perceptive history teacher, Mildred Scrivener, who cajoled him into participating in the school's Minstrel Show on 9th April,

Presley: the eternal legend.

1953. He received a tremendous reception when he sang *Keep Them Cold Icy Fingers Off of Me* and then did *Old Shep* as an encore. By the end of the performance the student audience went wild with applause.

Remembers Scrivener: "I'll never forget the look on his face when he came off stage. 'They really like me!' he beamed and all but wept."

Particularly impressed was one Dixie Locke. Petite and brunette, with a sweetness Elvis found both appealing and accessible, she became his first girlfriend. They began dating in the second semester of their junior year in 1953. The attractive, socially adept Locke was instrumental in boosting Presley's confidence and getting him to open up.

Remembers Greenwood: "Elvis was more himself around Dixie than any girl before or since, and happier. He walked on air in her presence. She was a direct contrast to Gladys, quiet with a soft voice and sparkling eyes. Elvis sensed a familiar vulnerability in her, and that drew them together."

Gladys Presley, however, viewed the schoolgirl as a threat to her own relationship with Elvis and remained haughty and aloof whenever Dixie's name was mentioned. "You'll be leavin' your mama all alone to live your own life somewhere," she wailed to Elvis in tears. "Promise you won't leave me!"

Greenwood remembers a visit to the Presley home just after Dixie had ended the relationship: "Elvis was sprawled on the couch looking pathetic. Gladys sat next to him, stroking his head, smoothing back the strands of his hair, looking satisfied, almost smug. 'Just you remember, nobody loves you like I do.'"

Broken-hearted, Elvis immersed himself in music. He began participating in late night gospel sings at Ellis Auditorium, a showcase for the primitive, urgent style of the Blackwood Brothers and the flamboyant Statesmen (who were to sing at Presley's funeral). Presley faithfully listened to Memphis WDIA, 'America's Only 50,000 Watt Negro Radio Station' and the first black station in the south, pouring out a blend of blues, gospel, and heavy driving R&B from the ghetto. Here Elvis familiarized himself with and was heavily influenced by artists such as Clyde McPhatter, Big Joe Turner and the outrageous fire and ice gospel vocalist, Sister Rosetta Tharpe, who wrote *Saved*, which Presley sang on his 1968 TV special, 'Elvis'.

But it was during his frequent visits to cobblestone Beale Street, near the docks of the Mississippi, that Elvis gained his real musical education. The birthplace of W.C. Handy's St. Louis Blues, Beale Street offered a raucous round of social clubs and honky tonks with patrons "stompin' the daylight into the flo." He especially liked hanging around black bluesmen such as B.B. King.

"I knew Elvis before he was popular," said King. "He used to come around us a lot. People had pawnshops there and a lot of us used to hang out in these places and this was where I met him."

By the late forties things were looking up for the Presley family. Vernon landed a steady job driving a truck while Gladys had gone to work as a nurse's aid. The family moved into a public housing project, the Lauderdale Courts, a step up for the Presleys. Elvis had several part-time jobs, including one as an usher at Loews State Theater for $17.50 a week until he was fired for punching a fellow usher who had snitched on a candy girl for giving Elvis free goodies.

To the delight of his proud parents, Elvis graduated in June 1953. He promptly got a job driving a truck for the Crown Electric Company for $35 a week while studying nights to be an electrician.

But as Elvis later joked, "Somehow I got short-circuited along the way."

Just around the corner his big break was waiting. Appropriately, it would all come about from a birthday present for his mother.

CHAPTER TWO

GOD'S GIFT

"I'm not kiddin' myself, my voice alone is just an ordinary voice. What people come to see is how I use it. If I stand still while I'm singin' I'm dead, man. I might as well go back to drivin' a truck."

Elvis Presley

Above and opposite: Presley at the start of 'Presleymania'.

WE RECORD ANYTHING ANYWHERE ANYTIME read the sign above the Memphis Recording Service, 706 Union Avenue, home of the fledgling Sun Records founded in 1952. Presley had passed it hundreds of times on his truck route, imagining what his voice would sound like on a real record.

In the late summer of 1953 Presley was searching for a gift idea for his mother's birthday (although it was some months past) and decided the time was finally right to record his voice. With the $4 recording fee in hand, Elvis went to the studio in his lunch hour to record his two chosen songs, *My Happiness* and *That's When Your Heartaches Begin* (a hit for the popular black trio, The Ink Spots, in 1950).

"Who do you sound like?" asked secretary, Marion Keisker, leading Elvis into the recording booth.

"I don't sound like nobody," he shot back.

Presley was very disappointed with his performance. "I was terrible. My guitar sounded like someone beatin' on a bucket lid or somethin'."

As Keisker played the tape back, however, the high plaintive voice captured her attention. This could be just what her boss was looking for. Sam Phillips, a former radio station engineer and disc jockey turned promoter and producer, rejected the type of material produced by stars such as Doris Day and Frankie Avalon in favor of the fresh, raw sound of rhythm and blues.

"It seemed to me that the negroes were the only ones who had any freshness left in their music," he later observed. "If I could find a white boy who had the negro sound and feel, I could make a million dollars."

Phillips listened to the anonymous "kid with the sideburns" and instantly realized the potential: "When I heard him, I thought, 'Here's an unpolished voice that really makes contact.' I don't know how I felt it, but somehow I did. There was no doubt he was going to be big." Phillips

An early recording session in Nashville.

filed away the tape together with 10 inch acetates of *Casual Love Affair* and *I'll Never Stand in Your Way*, which Elvis recorded in January, 1954. In June, 1954, Sam Phillips needed a demo singer for a ballad and remembered that dynamic, young voice.

Elvis ran all the way to the studio, but his hopes were promptly dashed when he was unable to master the sophisticated ballad, *Without You*. He tried a number of different songs, some of them copied from his current idol, Dean Martin, but at this point it appeared that he was simply not cut out for a recording career.

Bitterly disappointed Elvis trudged home, admitting, "I was just awful. It was a pretty enough song, but I just couldn't get a hold of it. It was so humiliating. Nobody would look me in the eye. I wanted to run outta there and not look back."

But Phillips wasn't quite ready to give up on his promising discovery. A few months later, on 5th July, 1954, Elvis was called back into the studio; this time, with a back-up combo of guitarist, Scotty Moore, and slap bassist, Bill Black, known for their outrageous 'hillbilly' sound. The begin-

In the cutting room of Sun Records.
Left to right: Presley, Bill Black, Scotty Moore and Sam Phillips.

ning of the recording session was not successful. *Harbor Lights* was barely acceptable and the sentimental country ballad, *I Love You Because* was terrible.

Then it happened. To relieve the tension during a break, Elvis began fooling around with Arthur 'Big Boy' Crudup's 1946 electric blues number, *That's All Right (Mama)*. Moore found the key and laid down a sizzling lead guitar while Black supplied a thumping bass line.

Phillips burst from the control room, shouting, "What the devil are you doing?"

"Just goofing off," replied Presley.

"Well get it figured out, quick. We've gotta get this on tape!"

The record was completed on the fourth take and Phillips knew he had found just what he wanted - a revolutionary mix of country and blues (which would later be called rockabilly). It could be said that 5th July, 1954, was the day that rock'n'roll was officially born.

Phillips peddled the song around town and found a taker in fast-talking hillbilly DJ, Dewey Phillips, at the all black station WHBQ. As soon as *That's All Right (Mama)* hit the airwaves on 7th July, 1954, the phone lines lit up. The blitz for requests was so overwhelming that Dewey played the song fourteen times that evening in his show, 'Red Hot and Blue' and Presley came down to the station for his first interview.

Sun Records received 7,000 orders for the record and Presley was immediately booked into Overton Park Shell in Memphis on 30th July as the opening act for established country artist Slim Whitman. Throwing his entire energy into the performance, complete with his famous stage gyrations, he played *That's All Right (Mama)* and *Blue Moon of Kentucky* and brought the house down. This was the start of 'Presleymania'.

A rare poster advertising an early gig.

Elvis with radio personality Dewey Phillips. Phillips was the very first DJ to play one of Elvis' songs on the radio.

According to Red West, "He was Marlon Brando and James Dean rolled into one. Elvis washed over the younger crowds and they got swept away. Elvis was theirs. He wasn't a hand-me-down from another generation, he was theirs."

Presley's recollection, however, was marked by less bravura: "I came out on stage and was scared stiff. It was my first big appearance in front of an audience. Everybody was hollerin' and I didn't know why. When I came off stage my manager told me it was because I was wigglin' my legs. The more I did, the louder it got."

Although his debut was an unequivocal success, subsequent performances proved discouraging. One particular appearance on 2nd

Opposite: Elvis 'the Pelvis' live and in person at the Florida Theater, Jacksonville in 1956.

THE ELVIS PRESLEY SHOW

STARRING

IN PERSON

ELVIS PRESLEY

WITH AN **ALL STAR CAST**

THE JORDONAIRES

PHIL MARAQUIN

FRANKIE CONNORS

BLUE MOON BOYS & Others

RCA Victor Recording Star

HEAR HIM SING
"HEARTBREAK HOTEL"
"HOUND DOG"
AND HIS OTHER GREAT
RECORDING HITS

FLORIDA THEATRE

JACKSONVILLE - FLORIDA

FRI · SAT AUG 10 - 11

MATINEE AND NIGHT SHOWS

Top: Elvis in 1956 looking pretty damn cool behind the wheel of his famous pink Cadillac.

Below: With fans at the Presley home at 1034 Audubon Drive in Memphis.

Opposite: Striking a dramatic pose.

October by the Blue Moon Boys (given the name by their manager, Bob Neal) at Nashville's vaunted Grand Ole Opry was a humiliating failure. The conservative, family-oriented audience stared in mute bewilderment at the figure center stage, dressed in flamboyant garb and pompadour. "I was shocked when I saw he was wearing eye shadow," recalls Chet Atkins. Jim Denny, the Opry's talent co-ordinator advised, "If I were you, son, I'd go back to truck driving."

Greenwood recalls Elvis' terrible disappointment: "He picked up a large board and suddenly began smashing it violently to the ground, cursing and crying, sinking to his knees in despair, 'I'm just not good enough. They're all gonna be laughing at me behind my back. How could I have been so stupid thinkin' I was gonna make somethin' special of myself!'"

Nonetheless, he managed to pull himself up and enlisted the management of Memphis DJ, Bob Neal, who booked him on a steady, if less than impressive circuit of clubs, fairs, outdoor concerts and even school proms. Neal was responsible for polishing his artist's image, trading in Elvis' beat-up Cadillac for a brand new Chevrolet. He also eliminated the loud and garish stage garb for the more brooding and mysterious solid black. "My 'outlaw of love' clothes," Presley called them.

Still a relatively obscure performer, Presley's next two singles, *Good*

With songwriters Leiber and Stoller.

Opposite: Elvis with Mae Axton, co-writer of *Heartbreak Hotel*.

Rockin' Tonight and *Milkcow Blues Boogie*, failed to chart. This dented his confidence and, at this time, he was seriously considering packing it in and returning to truck driving.

Then, over the winter of 1954-1955 Elvis got a break in the popular 'Hank Snow Jamboree' tour, where he attracted the attention of the self-styled 'Colonel' Thomas A. Parker. Born in Breda, Holland, in 1909, Parker (original name Van Kuijk) was a crafty, fast-talking carnival barker who had become the manager of stars such as Hank Snow and Eddy Arnold. Parker's keen eye took in the combination of raw talent mixed with Presley's sultry, olive-skinned good looks, and he smelled success.

Parker quickly realised that the road to Elvis was through his doting mother. Although she disliked him on sight, Parker's smooth-talking line of big plans for her baby boy soon won over Ma Presley and the first Parker/Presley contract was signed on 15th August, 1955.

Parker's input soon paid dividends. He booked his client into larger venues throughout the south and selected *Baby Let's Play House* as Presley's next single. This became Presley's first record to make the charts, reaching number ten on Billboard's country chart in July, 1955.

This was followed up by the great *Mystery Train*, which entered the country charts in September, 1955, staying there for thirty-one weeks

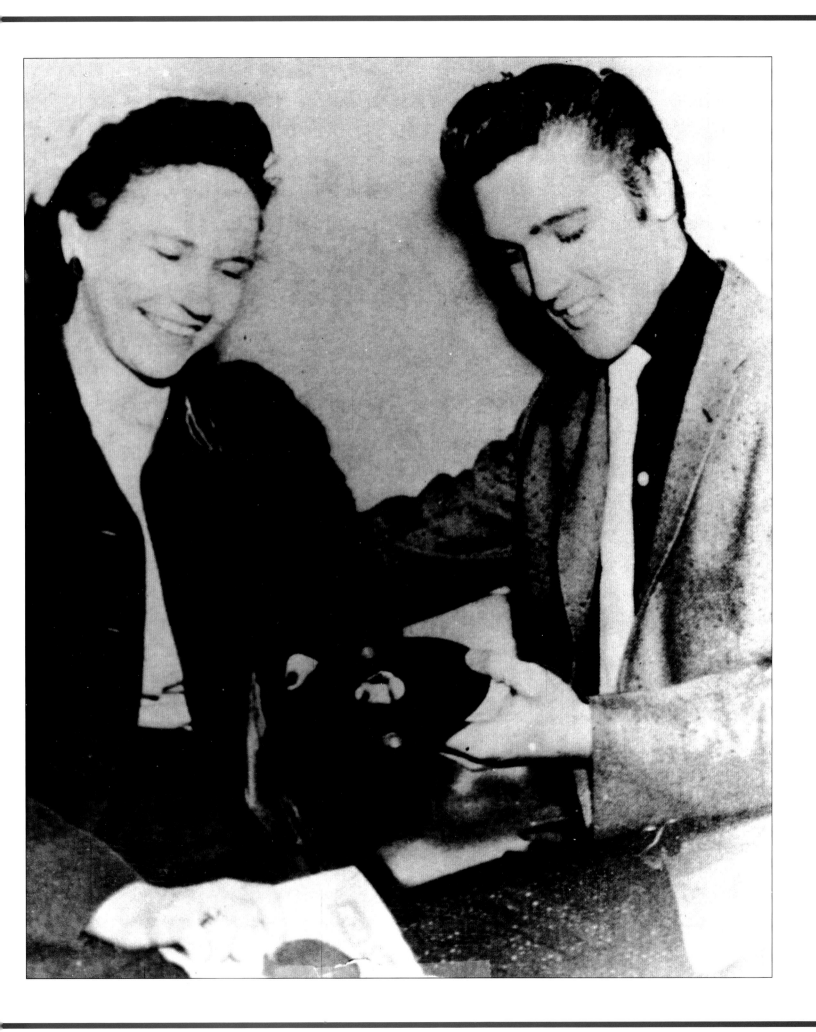

Relaxing in a Hollywood restaurant.
Left to right: 'Colonel' Tom Parker, actor
Robert Wagner and Presley.

Opposite: Presley looking rather bored in yet
another predictable publicity shot.

and eventually reaching number one. On 15th October Elvis played the
Cotton Club in Lubbock, Texas. The warm-up act was Buddy and Bob,
featuring nineteen-year-old Buddy Holly.

November, 1955 marked a monumental stepping-stone in Presley's
career, when RCA Victor purchased Elvis' contract from Sun Records in a
$40,000 deal. Elvis also signed a new contract with Tom Parker, which
gave the Colonel 25% of all of Presley's earnings and made him his
"sole and exclusive advisor, personal representative and manager." In
short, the Colonel owned Elvis, body and soul.

1956 became the year of Elvis with the release of *Heartbreak Hotel* in
January, written by Mae Axton and Tommy Durden and based on the
story of a suicide which appeared in *The Miami Herald*. The throaty
blues and rock number, with a bellowing echo and a searing guitar
break, presented Elvis as both saint and sinner. To the generation coming of age in the fifties, raised in the ultra-conservative boredom of crew
cuts, a granite-faced Eisenhower and bland heart-throb Pat Boone, this
explosion of unbridled pathos and passion struck a collective nerve.

In April *Heartbreak Hotel* became America's number one single and
stayed in that position for two months. Ringmaster Parker was there to

Mr. and Mrs Presley outside the Presley homestead in Audubon Drive, Memphis - the first house that Elvis bought.

Opposite: "You're looking for trouble, you've come to the right place!"

oversee it all in a carefully orchestrated campaign that produced an overnight blitz of Elvis merchandise, including Elvis soda, lunch-boxes and even pajamas. Within six months 400,000 teenagers joined the Elvis Presley Fan Club in the USA. Girls even cut their hair like 'the King' fashioning mock sideburns out of love for their idol.

As rock critic, Nick Cohn, observed: "Before Elvis, rock had been only a gesture, a vague rebellion. Once he happened, it immediately became solid, self-contained, spawning its own style in clothes and language."

Presleymania was swept along on the explosive tidal wave of the relatively new medium of television. Parker made sure that his client was booked on all the major TV variety shows, including 'The Milton Berle Show', 'The Steve Allen Show' and the Dorsey Brothers' 'Stage Show'. By the time Presley scored his greatest coup, a 9th September appearance on 'The Ed Sullivan Show', Sullivan had to offer $50,000 for a three-show deal. Ironically it was the Sullivan show that capped Presley's meteoric rise to fame and fortune, as the impresario had initially refused to book the singer, calling him "unfit for a family audience."

As a concession to family values, Ed instructed the cameramen to shoot Elvis only from the waist up. "That was kind of silly," said Presley. "It

didn't work. Didn't they know I just naturally have to jump around when I sing?"

The historic appearance delivered a whopping 82.6 Trendex rating, only exceeded eight years later by The Beatles.

Although fifty-four million viewers hailed the newly crowned king of rock'n'roll, he drew blistering notices from media critics. *The Washington Post* wrote, "That Elvis is kind to his parents isn't a free ticket to behave like a sex maniac in public before millions of impressionable kids." *New York Times* music critic, Jack Gould stated: "Mr. Presley has no discernible singing ability. His one specialty is an accentuated movement of the body that heretofore has been primarily identified with the repertoire of the blonde bombshells of burlesque." *Look* Magazine put it even more bluntly: "Presley's fame is overshadowed by a nightmare of bad taste. His gyrations, his nose wiping, his leers are vulgar."

In many places the bemused and resentful powers-that-be did their best

Above: The Presley family at the beginning of Elvis' rapid rise to fame.

Inset: Hanging tough at Audubon Drive.

Opposite: A candid shot in the backyard of Elvis' Memphis home.

Posing at the groovy gates of Graceland.

to shut out rock'n'roll music and the man who epitomized it. San Antonio banned rock music from being played at the city's public swimming pools. In Ottawa, eight students were expelled from the Notre Dame Convent School for attending a Presley concert. In Asbury Park, New Jersey (later the home of famous Elvis fan, Bruce Springsteen) all rock concerts were banned after twenty-five "vibrating teenagers" were hospitalized following a record hop. The height of absurdity came in Washington DC, where erstwhile teen idol, Frank Sinatra testified before a congressional committee: "Rock'n'roll is the most brutal, ugly, desperate, vicious form of expression it has been my misfortune to hear."

This, of course, was exactly what America's teens were looking for; if their parents didn't dig it, it had to be good! Hysteria reigned as Elvis toured the country. In New Orleans six girls bound and gagged an elevator operator and captured Elvis, holding him prisoner between floors for an hour. In Jacksonville, Presley closed the show by joking, "Girls, I'll see you all backstage." The invitation sent 14,000 nubile adolescents crashing through police barricades to tear at his clothes.

Overnight Elvis had become a very wealthy man. As Colonel Parker smugly declared, "When I met Elvis, he had a million dollars' worth of talent. Now he has a million dollars!"

Above: Elvis and his parents meet the press.
Inset: Yet another movie magazine pic.
Overleaf: Presley with his trusty six string acoustic.

A passionate moment from the movie *Stay Away Joe.*

In May, 1956, the Presleys moved (they had resided at four addresses since 1949) to a family home on Audubon Drive. Elvis added a $25,000 swimming pool and filled the garage with the finest cars money could buy. "When I was a kid," he revealed, "I'd sit out on our porch and watch those long, low cars whizz by. I told myself that when I was grown I was gonna have not one, but two Cadillacs sittin' out in front of Mama and Daddy's house." In September he bought his mother a pink Cadillac.

In November, 1956, Elvis' movie career began with the premiere of his *Love Me Tender,* a civil war piece co-starring Debra Paget. The movie was hastily made for one million dollars, and was universally panned by critics. On top of that, when devoted fans learned of Clint Reno's (Presley's part) demise in the film, they picketed theaters and petitioned the studio for a reprieve. In response, Elvis was shot in close-up singing the title song with his face superimposed over the final scene. Paramount recouped its costs five times over; Elvis on celluloid proved as big a hit as on record.

The following year, 1957, brought even greater success. With two

Left: Elvis with Loving You co-stars Dolores
Hart and Lizabeth Scott.
Below: With Dolores Hart.

more films (*Loving You* and *Jailhouse Rock*) grossing another ten million,
Elvis was a bonafide movie star. A pair of cross country tours added to
the coffers, while on record he had a further string of Billboard number
one hits.

RCA's Director of Operations, Steve Sholes, evolved Presley's raw and
lean rockabilly style at Sun into a fatter, more complex sound by adding
session musicians to the Presley line-up, including fabled guitarist, Chet
Atkins, and the gospel vocal back-up group, The Jordanaires. Sholes
transformed the Mississippi hillbilly into an eclectic artist as capable of
handling the ballad, *Love Me Tender* as the rough and ready, *Don't Be
Cruel*.

Asked if he ever considered voice lessons, Presley grinned, "Not me.
I'm not taking any chances. They just might train that thing right out of
my throat!"

In March of 1957 Presley purchased from Mrs Ruth Browne Moore the
house that was to become the most celebrated home in rock'n'roll,
Graceland. The 1939, eighteen room, fieldstone fronted, antebellum
mansion perched on fourteen hilltop acres in suburban Whitehaven was

Left: The famous Presley crooked smile.
Above: With *King Creole* love interest Carolyn Jones.

in a poor state of repair when Elvis paid the $102,500 purchase price. Over the next six months he would spend another half million dollars renovating and improving, from the custom designed iron gates bearing his musical insignia, to the ostentatious, garish interiors boasting a mirrored dining table, purple wallpaper, stained glass peacocks, to an all-black bedroom suite and the famous Jungle Room with its green ceiling rugs and seven-foot hand-carved island god thrones.

"A black hole in the aesthetic universe designed by the same A-bomb sensibility that had detonated American music," writer Jane Stern called it.

As 1958 approached, Elvis and his family were installed in their dream house watching the money roll in. Nothing, it seemed, could disturb their universe. Nothing, that is, except Uncle Sam.

Opposite: An early sixties shot.

CHAPTER THREE

MAMA'S BOY

"If I could have one wish it would be to talk with my mother again. There are times I dream about her. She's always happy and smiling. Sometimes we embrace. It's so real I wake up in a cold sweat."

Elvis Presley

Above: Private Presley following his induction in the United States Army.

Opposite: Getting ready for an inspection.

ON 24TH MARCH, 1958, Elvis exchanged his blue suede shoes for a pair of combat boots and became Private Presley, Serial Number 53310761. He had received his draft notice just before Christmas the previous year and was originally supposed to enter the army on 20th January, but was fortunate enough to obtain a couple of months deferment. Never had an inductee attracted such attention. His arrival in Fort Chaffee, Arkansas was attended by crowds of ardent fans and representatives from the international media. 'A Star is Shorn!' blasted headlines as Presley's ducktail was shaved off by James Peterson, a civilian barber, for 65 cents. Fans were horrified to learn that the famous locks would be burned according to army practice. One enterprising individual offered Parker $500,000 for Elvis' shorn locks, but the Colonel was unable to get through the army red tape to do the deal.

Parker regretted that his boy was forgoing so much income by joining the service, but, at the same time, viewed Elvis' military stint as a superb opportunity to showcase him as the classic all-American, eager to fulfil his sacred duty to God and country.

"I'm going into the service to do the best I can," stated a compliant Elvis. "If they want me to sing for the boys I'll sing. If they want me to march, anything they want me to do is all right." In fact, Presley was glad for a rest from the brutal pace of the past two years. "It'll be a relief. It won't be a snap, but it'll give me a chance to unwind and catch my breath."

In reality there was no way Elvis could ever be a normal GI. Unlike the other recruits doing basic training with the Second Armored Division at Fort Hood, Texas, and living in the barracks, Presley rented a home in nearby Killeen for his family and whizzed around the base in a bright

Above: Posing with a Memphis fan.

red Lincoln convertible. Anita Wood, a Memphis disc jockey and singer, and Elvis' girlfriend at the time, would often join the Presley family in Killeen.

Gladys Presley, her health in decline for some ten years, was now deteriorating rapidly. She was spending entire days in bed with chills, her skin a deathly yellow with dark, hollow circles beneath her eyes. Her emotional state probably contributed to the deterioration in her health. She was desperately concerned about being parted from her son when he received his final orders to be shipped overseas.

Despite her serious condition, Presley, reassured by Vernon, convinced himself that his mother was merely suffering from heat exhaustion and was confident that her return to Memphis would soon see her restored to good health.

Back home, Gladys was rushed to the hospital and diagnosed as suffer-

Left: A snapshot of Elvis in his army uniform taken by an admirer.

Above: Presley chatting with fans while he was stationed in Germany.

ing from severe hepatitis. Several combinations of medication proved fruitless and her condition got worse. Her weak heart, burdened by her excessive weight, coupled with a liver bloated from years of alcohol abuse was not equal to the struggle. Granted emergency leave, Elvis took the first plane back to Memphis and raced to his mother's room. His mother, too weak even to sip from a glass, was obviously gravely ill.

Presley stayed at his mother's side for some thirty-six hours, and, on the evening of 13th August, Gladys roused herself to speak to her son. "I'm tired honey. All I want to do is sleep. If you're here I'll want to stay awake. I mean it son. Don't make me have to ask you again, okay?"

Observed Greenwood, "It wasn't like Gladys to be so insistent about Elvis not spending time with her. She said goodbye to him, her eyes filled with intense emotion, staring at Elvis as if she knew she'd never see him again."

Elvis in his dashing dress uniform with Vernon.

Opposite: Arriving for his tour of duty in Germany in September, 1958.

Presley reluctantly went out and watched a movie. On his return to Graceland he got a call from Vernon. Gladys Presley had died of a heart attack at 3.00 am, 14th August at the age of forty-six.

Predictably, Elvis' reaction was intensely emotional. As Gladys' body was laid out in the music room, he threw himself on the coffin, stroking her, combing her hair and clutching a pink housecoat he'd given her. By the day of the funeral he was in an almost delirious state, falling upon the casket wailing, "Don't leave me Mama. I did everything for you, it was all for you. Give me another chance and I'll do better, I promise!"

Her body was buried at Forest Hill Cemetery and the Blackwood Brothers sang at the funeral service. Following the burial, Presley locked himself away for nine days, rambling on about tearing down Graceland and moving away. "He harbored incredible anger at Gladys for leaving him alone in this world," recalls Greenwood. "She'd left him and gone to Jesse, whom Elvis always believed was her preferred son. No matter what he did, he could never get away from the shadow of his brother."

Above: Staring down the barrel of a bazooka somewhere out in the field.
Left: Sharing a bite with fourteen-year-old Priscilla while still in Germany in 1959.

Still mourning, Elvis left Fort Hood with his unit by train on 19th September en route for Brooklyn New York and his tour of duty in Friedberg near Frankfurt, West Germany. There he was met by hordes of frauleins who crashed through police cordons to get a precious glimpse of their idol. Once again, Elvis put up family and friends, including his grandmother, Minnie Mae Hood, his father and several buddies who would form the nucleus of the famous 'Memphis Mafia', in a three-storey home in nearby Bad Nauheim. There, aside from the occasional exuberant party, Presley spent his free time reading poetry and mastering karate (in which he eventually earned an eighth degree black belt).

As for his army duty, he proved to be an excellent soldier, quickly rising to the rank of sergeant in January, 1960, and displaying his superior marksmanship with a rifle.

Opposite: Signing for a fan.

Elvis and the Colonel going over a few details.

Opposite: Elvis' *Love Me Tender* look.

In the closing months of 1959, Presley encountered what he called "my destiny". US Airman Currie Grant brought a petite, stunning girl to an off-base party. Priscilla Beaulieu, the adopted daughter of an Air Force officer, was fourteen years old when she met Elvis Presley.

"She's an angel," Presley breathlessly exclaimed. Introducing himself, he asked her if she attended school.

"Ninth," she replied.

"Ninth what?" Elvis asked, rather confused.

"Ninth grade."

"Why you're just a baby," he remarked, grinning.

Presley was so taken with the teenager that he began seeing her on a regular basis. A twenty-five-year-old rock star dating a fourteen-year-old schoolgirl, however, was potentially dangerous, so the couple conducted a discreet relationship with country picnics and romantic dinners, along with the odd cuddle in his room.

On 2nd March Elvis left Germany by plane for the US, stopping briefly at Prestwick Airport in Scotland - the only time he was to set foot in

Elvis and Earl Greenwood at Union Station in Memphis on 18th April, 1960.

Opposite: Making eyes at the camera, as only Elvis can.

Britain. Elvis was honorably discharged from the army in 1960, at Fort Dix in the midst of a howling blizzard with thousands of fans standing knee deep in snow to welcome him home. With accrued royalties of $1.3 million waiting for him, he was clearly not forgotten.

Presley seemed ready to take up right where he left off, with an appearance on The Frank Sinatra Timex Special 'Welcome Home Elvis', which aired on ABC TV on 12th May, 1960. Sinatra, who had earlier been very critical of Elvis, apparently had a change of heart when he saw the chance to improve his slipping TV ratings. Presley was paid $125,000 for the guest spot, by far the highest figure in the history of broadcasting. But something wasn't right. Elvis, dressed in a tux warbling *Witchcraft* wasn't exactly rock'n'roll. *The New York Times* described the performance as, "Nothing morally reprehensible, it was merely awful."

As he headed back to Hollywood to film his first post-army film, *GI Blues,* Elvis was distinctly unhappy. Looking over the script, he threw it down in disgust. "I ain't out of the army a week and they wanna put me right back in. This is a joke. I feel like a damn idiot breaking into a song while I'm talking to some chick on a train."

Presley had at last begun to question Parker's management. Unhappy over the songs RCA selected for his next album, he told the manager,

"They're making enough money off me, the least they can do is let me sing a couple of songs that make me feel good."

"You don't tamper with success," countered Colonel Tom. "The time's not right."

"I don't see why I have to keep waitin'."

"Stop being difficult Elvis," barked Parker. "Maybe later."

But later, unfortunately, would never come.

Nevertheless Elvis' recordings continued to dominate the record charts, with *It's Now or Never* and *Are You Lonesome Tonight* both going to number one in the USA and the UK.

Meanwhile, back at Graceland, Elvis returned to find a disturbing turn of events; another woman had taken his mother's place. Davada (Dee) Stanley was the young wife of an army sergeant with whom Vernon had been conducting a clandestine affair in Germany, carefully kept secret from his son. To Elvis, who had pictured his father as the grieving widower, this was a rather devastating shock. He could not understand how Vernon could so easily and rapidly replace Gladys while her things were still hanging in the closet and her perfume lingered in the house.

This development couldn't have come at a worse time for the father-son relationship. Elvis had been forging a tentative bond of trust with his father, following many years of anger and resentment at

Enjoying a rare day off at a Memphis amusement park in July, 1960.

Vernon's frequent absences, his brushes with the law and his allowing Gladys to fend for the family. His mother's last wish to "keep the family together" seemed to be happening. Now this sudden betrayal, a new mistress of Graceland.

Earl Greenwood recalls: "As the news sank in Elvis threw a tantrum of frightening proportions that brought his neighbors running outside. He hurled furniture at the walls and left holes with his fists."

Dee, who married Vernon on 3rd July, 1960, in Huntsville, Alabama, paints a very different account of their relationship: "Elvis told me, 'Dee, I want you to consider this your home too. This place belongs to you now as much as it does to me and Daddy.' I had to earn his respect, but soon we grew to like each other fine. Then it grew into real respect and love, until one day Elvis told me that it was destiny that brought me and my sons into the family."

At the close of the fifties it seemed that even rock's founder, the king himself, with his sideburns shorn, black leathers discarded, the hip swivel all but hammered out of him, had abdicated the throne. "The army finally made a man out of him," people were beginning to say.

Embraced by the establishment, the universal death knell for rebels of every generation, Presley would move on, but the fire was gone. As a new decade unfolded the fiery rock'n'roll period of his career was over.

Opposite: Those famous good looks .....

CHAPTER FOUR

INTO THE FIRE

"I don't regard money or position as important, but I can never forget the longing to be someone. I guess if you're poor, you always think bigger and want more than fellows who have most everything from the minute they're born."

Elvis Presley

BY THE BEGINNING OF 1961 the irascible Colonel Parker moved into phase two of his master plan to make Elvis a movie star. It was no secret that he disdained rock'n'roll, considering it just another passing fad. As part of his plan to wean his client away from rock he, allegedly, squeezed out Presley's faithful musicians, Scotty Moore and Bill Black, by paying them a mere $200 a week, forcing them to pay their own touring expenses and granting them no royalties. By the time Elvis returned to the studio in March, 1961, Moore and Black, fed up with Parker's tactics, quit in a huff, although Moore did continue to play with Elvis on and off for a number of years.

Parker also saw to it that Presley played a Hawaiian benefit concert on 25th March to raise money for the USS Arizona Memorial Fund. Country singer Minnie Pearl, on board for the event observed, "Elvis never got out of his room except to work. He couldn't come out during the day. He had a penthouse suite and we'd look up and Elvis would be standing at the window, looking down at us. Years later, as word filtered down of Elvis' unhappiness and seeming withdrawal, I would think of that day in Hawaii. No wonder he lost touch with reality."

All that remained for Parker to do was to play on Presley's love for the movies, and, more importantly, his insecurity which was the result of a lifetime of poverty. With Gladys gone, the Colonel soon took her place as the dominant force in Presley's life.

"I don't know how long the music end of it will go, but movies are forever," Elvis was telling the public.

The last of the rebel Elvis was effectively quashed with the 1961 blockbuster success of *Blue Hawaii*, with its accompanying soundtrack album, which eventually sold more than five million copies. Originally titled,

Opposite: Presley, circa 1960.

Elvis always had to have a woman around him ....

Beach Boy, the musical ushered in eight years of indifferent Presley pictures, whose unvarying formula featured the ever virtuous, always frolicsome Elvis surrounded by starlets and with a full complement of dim-witted tunes.

These films were cranked out on a shoestring budget, usually in a period of three or four weeks, but many of them grossed five million dollars or more. Parker, uninterested in the plot, would tell the directors, "Go ahead and make your movie, all we want is songs for an album."

The Colonel's cavalier attitude was responsible for Elvis making some major career blunders. The greatest of these resulted from the Colonel's advice to Elvis not to consider the role of Tony in *West Side Story*, opposite Natalie Wood. In Presley, the cinematic community spotted an excit-

Left: Out on the town with teen movie sensation Natalie Wood.

Above: On the set of the film *Flaming Star*.

Clowning with piano man Liberace.

ing, raw talent that could have been developed much more successfully, given the right vehicles.

Nicholas Ray, director of *Rebel Without A Cause*, wanted Presley to star in the *James Dean Story*. Robert Mitchum thought him perfect for *Thunder Road*. Years later Barbra Streisand offered Presley the co-starring role in *A Star is Born*. But to Colonel Tom, the idea of Presley playing outlaws, weak-willed alcoholics or, indeed, any type of moral outcast was completely out of the question.

Confined to the inanity of B-movies, Elvis' acting potential was never fully realized. In a few more serious roles, however, critics did take notice. In 1960's *Flaming Star*, a psychological western with only two songs, Presley, in a role turned down by Brando, portrayed Pacer, a half breed Indian. Under the guidance of Don Siegel (*Invasion of the Body Snatchers, Dirty Harry*), one of the few class directors to take on a Presley film, Elvis competently displayed a range of inner torment, which prompted some people in the media to proclaim, "He can act!"

Unfortunately, the public, well trained to accept the singer in less challenging roles, preferred their hero softly crooning to a bevy of beauties and the film was not warmly received by Elvis fans. Parker always cited

this example whenever Elvis held out for meatier roles.

The few times when Elvis demanded creative control, the results demonstrated some ability and aptitude. *Jailhouse Rock's* famous dance sequence for instance, choreographed by Presley, demonstrated an electrifying and creative potential which was never to be fully explored.

The highest price for Elvis' mediocre screen stardom was paid in terms of his musical output. His last serious recording effort took place shortly after his discharge from the army in Nashville in April, 1960, and resulted in *Elvis is Back*, an amalgamation of creative pop with a sharp rock edge. But from 1961 onwards, when Elvis committed himself to Tom Parker's movie career, there was nothing but sound track albums and, sadly, he never got back to rock'n'roll. During his heyday as the king of rock, the world's finest songwriters were at his disposal, such as Otis Blackwell (*Don't Be Cruel*), Carl Perkins (*Blue Suede Shoes*) and Charles Calhoun (*Shake, Rattle And Roll*). Ironically, Elvis' huge success launched a rock revolution that spurred artists to record and perform their own material. The cult of the singer/songwriter left Elvis, who was no composer, hopelessly behind.

Top: A still from *Roustabout*, the closest thing to an action film that Elvis ever made.
Above: An impromptu autograph session.

Right: With Presley promotion king Pete Bennett.

Below: A scene from the movie *Easy Come Easy Go.*

However, Elvis and his contribution to rock were universally revered by the newer and younger stars. The Beatles were quick to pay homage. Said John Lennon: "The only person we wanted to meet in the United States was Elvis Presley. He was the thing. Before Elvis there was nothing."

Meanwhile, back on the home front, in the summer of 1962, Presley had moved his teenage girlfriend, Priscilla Beaulieu, into Graceland, ostensibly as the guest of Vernon and Dee. He managed to win over Priscilla's stern stepfather, Captain Joseph Beaulieu, by promising that she would be properly chaperoned by Vernon and Dee and that he would put his daughter through the finest school in Memphis, The Immaculate Conception High School.

Cool man Elvis cruising the streets.

Red West remembers her arrival: "I was in the kitchen at Graceland and I saw her there. Wow! Every bit as good as the build-up. The great thing about her was her easy manners. You always felt easy with her. She did look a lot older than fifteen and spoke a lot older, very sophisticated."

Elvis drove Priscilla to Immaculate Conception every morning and then expected her to stay up and party with him all night. This was duly accomplished with the aid of amphetamines and barbiturates, a practice Presley had adopted in the service to keep awake on sentry duty.

Recalled Priscilla: "It was a Dexedrine for him and one for me. I routinely took 'helpers' in order to get to sleep after wild rides at the fair-

grounds or early morning jam sessions. And I routinely took more 'helpers' when I woke up in order to maintain that fast pace and to study for my exams."

Acutely aware of Priscilla's status as a minor, Presley was, in fact, obsessed with keeping his future bride "virginal and pure". "He put me on a pedestal," revealed Beaulieu, "said he was saving me until the time was sacred and right." Instead, Elvis the film star redirected their passions in stimulating, but PG-rated homemade videotaped fantasies.

Presley's infatuation with the teenager may have been influenced by Priscilla's similarity to his mother. Physically, her brunette locks and striking blue eyes resembled the look of Gladys when she was young and attractive. Beyond that Priscilla's determined spirit and frank outspokenness reminded Elvis of his strongwilled mother.

There are some who claim that Presley saw in the beautiful young lady a female version of himself. This view was prompted by the outrageous fashion in which Elvis would make up his young queen with layers of false eyelashes, dyeing her hair the exact Clairol shade he used and then piling it up on her head in a ludicrous beehive. He completed the unusual look by dressing the teenager in sexy, clinging, sophisticated gowns.

The role of Elvis turned svengali may have been a reaction to years of maternal domination. Now he could turn the tables, moulding his young ward to his own beliefs and interests, including how to handle a firearm.

Below and opposite: Presley marries the lovely Priscilla Beaulieu on 1st May, 1967.

"While my classmates were wondering which college to apply to, I was deciding which gun to wear with what sequinned dress," laughed Priscilla.

"The Pygmalion nature of our relationship" she revealed, "was a mixed blessing. Elvis was my mentor, someone who studied my every gesture, listened critically to my every utterance and was generous to a fault with advice. The more we were together, the more I came to resemble him in every way. His tastes, his insecurities, his hang-ups all became mine."

There was yet another obvious benefit to her tender age: Presley was able to keep her at Graceland, while, in Hollywood, he romanced his glamorous co-stars, including Debra Paget, Tuesday Weld and Juliet Prowse.

As road manager, Joe Esposito, explained: "Elvis could not be a one woman man, no way. He always had to have a woman around him. When he was away from one he had to have somebody else there. That's just the way he was, I guess because of his mother."

Presley was able to dismiss tabloid stories of his affairs as studio publicity grist, until his heavily publicized affair with sex kitten Ann-Margaret on the set of *Viva Las Vegas*. "There was an immediate attraction between them that was passionate, intense and volatile," observed Greenwood. "Ann-Margaret was the kind of woman who brought out the best and worst in Elvis. Wanting to impress her, needing to feel worthy of her attention, he turned on the boyish charm and won her over with his sense of humor. But she was very independent, the type of female that frightened Elvis to death and made him feel inferior and threatened."

That inner conflict, asserts Greenwood, led to some of Presley's best emotional scenes on camera and made *Viva Las Vegas* his most successful motion picture and overall, his finest musical.

This time, however, Priscilla, now an astute eighteen-year-old, was furious. She stood up to Elvis, openly accusing him of infidelity and was horrified by his reaction. He flew into a rage, tore her clothes from the closet and demanded that she pack her bags and fly home to her parents. Just as abruptly he whirled her around and said, "Now do you understand? Do you see that you need this? You need someone to take you right to this point and put you in your place."

"What I didn't realize until later," she admitted, "was that this was Elvis' technique of keeping me under control."

Five years after Beaulieu had moved in with Presley, the couple married on 1st May, 1967. As usual, Parker handled the arrangements, shuffling friends and relatives about like circus acts. Instead of the glamorous showbiz wedding which the public was expecting, there was only a miserable eight minute ceremony at the Aladdin Hotel, a Las Vegas casino. However, there was a second marriage celebration for friends and employees at Graceland on 29th May.

Reporter Dirk Vellenga remembers: "The Colonel's patent mean-spiritedness was plainly at work. Once more he proved that a class act was something far beyond him."

But there was far more to it than that. "Elvis' world had been split into two distinct and often warring camps," added Vellenga. "On one side

Opposite: Presley as he appeared in the film *Love Me Tender*.

Time out for a meal.

there was Elvis, his father, Priscilla and his gang of cronies and retainers. The others were the Colonel's troops who basically believed that they made Elvis' money and resented the profligate spending that went on at Graceland. Following the wedding, the good ole boys were banished to the outer circle and the Colonel demonstrated that Elvis wasn't God and not even the star could tell the manager what to do."

On 1st February, 1968, nine months to the day after their wedding, Priscilla delivered Elvis' only child, Lisa Marie. The very image of her father, she was to become the most spoiled kid in the USA. Presley frequently rented entire amusement parks and roller rinks for her and gave her presents such as a slot machine and a fur coat at the age of nine.

Priscilla offers this insight: "By the time Lisa was four she realized she could manipulate the staff. Whenever one of them refused to do something for her she'd threaten, 'I'm gonna tell my daddy and you're going to be fired.' Since none of them wanted her going to Elvis, they'd let her have her way. The result was, Lisa had trouble learning right and wrong. Used to seeing people jump at her father's command, she took years to overcome this habit."

Freely lavishing his fortune on his family, Presley was certainly not one to squirrel it away. Aside from his renowned collection of automobiles (Elvis kept them lined up in the driveway, keys in the ignition, ready to roll), he owned no fewer than five airplanes, including the customized Convair jet, 'Lisa Marie', plus lavish homes in Bel Air, Palm Springs and the Circle G Ranch in Walls, Mississippi which stabled eighteen of the finest show horses money could buy.

Said West: "Elvis began by buying a horse and ended up buying the ranch, including trailers for a staff of nine and trucks for everyone. Vernon would just gasp when he got those bills. Elvis would laugh and say, 'Hell man, there is plenty more where that came from.'"

However, Presley didn't just spend his money on personal luxuries. He also relished the opportunity to play philanthropist to a host of worldwide charities, including the March of Dimes, the Muscular Dystrophy Foundation and Memphis' own St. Jude Hospital. At Christmas he routinely donated over $100,000 to aid the poor across the country. "Money's meant to be spread around," he asserted. "The more happiness it helps to create, the more it's worth. It's as worthless as an old cut-up paper if it just lays in the bank and grows there without ever having been used to help a body."

It is his countless, spontaneous acts of generosity to his fans that are most often remembered. Elvis once slipped off a $2,500 ring from his finger and gave it to an astonished eighteen-year-old admirer; he gave $500 to a blind man selling pencils on the streets of Memphis; he routinely gave away $1,000 bills, trips to Hawaii, even McDonalds certificates. But it was always the cars that claimed the most attention. Countless times, while visiting his favorite auto dealerships he purchased sports cars for lucky passers-by on the spot.

One time, recalls Dave Hebler, a member of Presley's retinue, he bought nine Lincolns for his staff: "It got even crazier the next day when he wanted to take them back and buy Cadillacs instead. Can you imagine the salesman's reaction when we all drove up in those Lincolns and said, 'Take them back'? The guy almost had a heart attack!"

Although his film career was financing his opulent lifestyle, by the end of the sixties, Elvis had grown tired of playing bland, one-dimensional characters and singing insipid tunes. "I keep getting offered the same old musicals, same story lines and they're getting worse and worse," he complained to Priscilla.

At last Elvis had had enough. Presley was about to relive, briefly, his earlier glory and to return to the charts in a blazing comeback.

CHAPTER FIVE

TAKING CONTROL

"I didn't feel like I could communicate with anybody, I felt terribly alone. I'm a number eight person, the thing that says they're intensely alone at heart. They hide their feelings in life and do what they please."

Elvis Presley

B Y 1968, the Colonel realized that Elvis needed something to kick-start his career. The movies he was making were ever more mediocre, with instantly forgettable productions such as *Double Trouble, Clambake, Stay Away Joe* and *Speedway* being banished to the drive-in circuit very soon after their release. It was becoming clear that the cinema was not going to sustain Presley's career, as 1969's offerings, the very poor pre-Eastwood western, *Charro*, and the frankly ludicrous *Change of Habit* (with Mary Tyler-Moore) made even more obvious.

The ever-resourceful Parker found the answer in a blockbuster television special for which he negotiated a huge million dollar deal with NBC. Colonel Tom had the format all figured out, a Christmas family show, with Elvis crooning holiday carols.

But a young, talented producer/director named Steve Binder had other ideas and wasn't about to be intimidated by the obstinate manager. "I felt very strongly that the special was Elvis' moment of truth. If he did another MGM movie on the special he would wipe out his career. On the reverse, if we could create an atmosphere of making Elvis feel he was creating the special himself, the same way he was originally involved in producing his records, people would really see Elvis Presley, not what the Colonel wanted them to see."

For the first time Presley stood up to the Colonel and agreed to return to his raw, rock'n'roll roots. On the day of taping, 27th June, 1968, at NBC's Studio 4 in Burbank, California, out swaggered Elvis, taut and lean, poured into black leather, snarling at the camera, once more cocky and dangerous. From the moment he launched into the double-barreled rocker, *Trouble* (by Leiber and Stoller from *King Creole*), the audience was by his side roaring its collective approval: The King was back!

Opposite: Elvis with his beloved daughter, Lisa Marie.

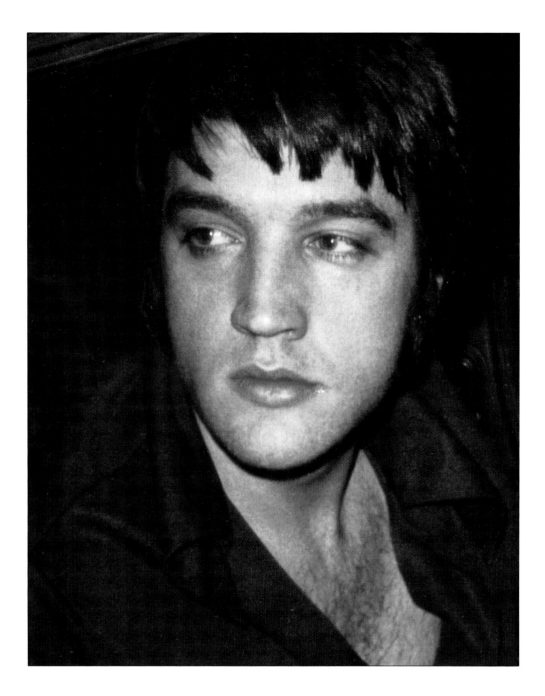

The material merged a careful blend of old and new: *Heartbreak Hotel, One Night, All Shook Up* and *Jailhouse Rock*, as well as the contemporary *Guitar Man* and *Nothingville*. The smouldering *Let Yourself Go* was so suggestive that it was cut from the final show, as were *It Hurts Me, Blue Suede Shoes, Don't Be Cruel* and *That's All Right (Mama)*. Backed by the old gang at Sun, including Scotty Moore and D.J. Fontana, the performance was a powerful reaffirmation of Presley's strength and soul. He virtually flew off stage beaming, "They still like me!"

Stepbrother, Rick Stanley, noted, "It was the most incredible thing to just see him suddenly there, look into the camera with that sly look and say, 'If you're looking for trouble you came to the right place!'"

Airing on 3rd December, the special was an unqualified success. Rock critic Greil Marcus hailed: "It was the finest music of his life. If there was ever music that bleeds, this was it. Nothing came easy that night and he

Presley's second family.
Left to right: Stepmother Dee, Elvis, his father
Vernon and stepbrother Rick.

gave everything he had, more than anyone knew he had."

Most significantly, for the first time since the very beginning, the effort was Presley's alone. For once, the Colonel had been excluded.

The triumph had to rank as the greatest jump-start to any career in recent memory. The special's finale, *If I Can Dream*, became Presley's first million seller in nearly a decade and stayed in the Billboard Hot 100 chart for thirteen weeks. Elvis was ready for more. Immediately he went into American Sound Studios, a black Memphis company whose artists included Aretha Franklin, and, in two bursts of recording activity in January and February, 1969, recorded the hit singles, *Kentucky Rain, Cry Daddy* and *The Wonder of You*. At this time he also recorded Mac Davis' stirring social commentary, *In The Ghetto*, which made it to number three in the USA and number two in the UK.

Once again, Parker was nearly responsible for another monumental blunder when he attempted to dissuade Elvis from recording Mark James' *Suspicious Minds*. Taking an immediate dislike to the song, he badgered Elvis, "Com'on, you don't need that song. We've already got *In The Ghetto* and *Kentucky Rain*. What do we need this one for!"

But Elvis dug in his heels and stood firm. "The old man's tampering with my music. He should stick to his deals and keep out of my music. I'll sing the songs I want, the way I hear them!"

Released in September, 1969, *Suspicious Minds*, with its powerful vocal, is the definitive record of Elvis at thirty-four, mature and in his prime. *Suspicious Minds* went to number one and stayed in the charts

for fifteen weeks. Elvis would never again have a number one record in the Hot 100 chart.

Shortly afterwards, Steve Binder approached the king with a concern: "My real feeling is that I don't know if you'll do any of the great things you want to do. Maybe the bed has been made already, maybe this'll be just a little fresh air you'll experience for a month."

"No I won't," he insisted. "From now on, I'm going to really do things."

But Binder's concerns were well founded. A humiliated Tom Parker knew that he had to take back the reins of power, and fast. Although Presley's latest material could best be described as soft rock, the Colonel feared he was edging too close to the arena now dominated by the likes of The Beatles, The Who, The Doors and Jimi Hendrix. No way would he allow Elvis to hit the road and once more become the leather-clad rebel he so detested.

Instead, Parker turned his attention to a new opportunity - Las Vegas. As it happened, two of Parker's cronies were running the brand new International Hotel (known as the Las Vegas Hilton since March, 1971), whose main showroom was about to be opened on 2nd July, 1969, by Barbra Streisand. The Colonel moved quickly, getting his client booked as the International's second star performer, taking out advertisements in all the trades and renting every available billboard to flash Elvis' name in neon across the desert sky. To his credit, he also put together a fine band, with a sexy gospel quartet and a superlative twenty-five piece orchestra.

His efforts paid off, as *Time, Newsweek* and *Rolling Stone*, along with the world's top journalists, made their way to Vegas to see Presley.

Presley arriving on the set of one of his many films.

On 31st July, 1969, Elvis emerged on stage, clad completely in black, to 2,000 screaming fans already standing on chairs and screaming their appreciation. Running through his early rock classics, adding his latest hits and even taking a few pages from The Beatles' songbook, with *Yesterday* and *Hey Jude*, Presley left the stage in triumph.

It was a critical and commercial success. *Variety* said, "A superstar, very much in command of the entire scene." *Rolling Stone* went even further, calling the experience "Supernatural, his own resurrection."

Parker, himself caught up in the hoopla, hastily negotiated a five million dollar contract scribbled on a tablecloth. But this time the usually shrewd

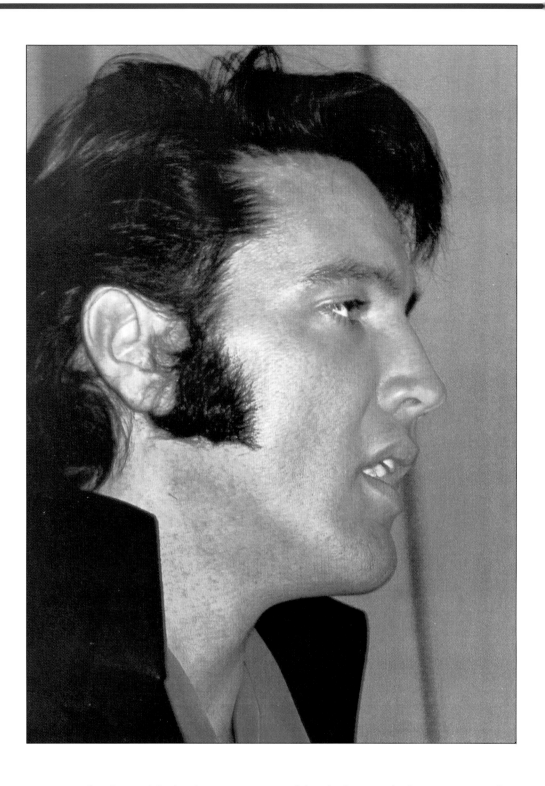

operator had stumbled. The International had obtained Elvis' services for eight weeks a year for the next five years and had just perpetrated the steal of the century. Elvis was to give a total of 350 performances at the Las Vegas Hilton before he died.

Both in Vegas and in the studio, Presley had begun to introduce more gospel material into his repertoire, culminating in the 1972 album entitled *He Touched Me*. His command of the genre stemmed from childhood influences and from a genuine heartfelt love for this spiritual music which came from somewhere deep within him. "Gospel music puts your mind to rest," he once commented.

Famous gospel singer, J.D. Sumner, had high praise for Presley's aptitude for spirituals. "Gospel music made Elvis what he was. He truly had a gift from God. You never heard anyone sing a gospel song like Elvis."

His mastery of gospel music was such that Presley's only Grammy awards came from his work in the sacred music field for *How Great Thou Art* (1967 Best Sacred Performance) and *He Touched Me* (1972 Best Inspirational Performance).

Presley's search for the spiritual side of life, however, extended far beyond music. Throughout his life Elvis was obsessed by the quest for something greater. A portable library of some two hundred spiritual

Surrounded by bodyguards following an electrifying performance. Vernon Presley is top right.

Elvis, always an intense performer.

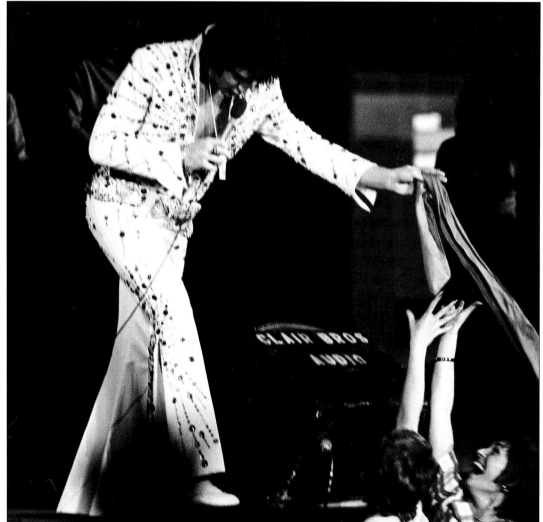

Elvis and his amazing bell bottoms!

books, including the Bible, the Dead Sea Scrolls and *The Prophet*,
accompanied him on all his travels. During his concerts fans would
sometimes hand him a Bible and Elvis would stop mid-performance to
quote favorite passages.

His intensity sometimes reached extremes. Priscilla recalls his bizarre
Bible readings in the den of their Bel Air home before a group of young
fans: "I sat next to him one evening as he read passages with great
force. Facing us were several of his female admirers wearing the lowest
cut blouses and the shortest mini skirts, disciples enraptured in the presence of their 'lord'."

"Sitting at his feet was an attractive, well-endowed, young girl wearing
a blouse unbuttoned to her navel. Leaning over seductively, she asked in
honeyed tones, 'Elvis, do you think the woman at the well was a vir-
gin?'"

"'Well, honey,' he said, 'I personally think Jesus was attracted to her!'"

Despite his deep respect for Christianity, Presley actively explored all
religions, from Buddhism to Scientology and even Pyramid Power. He

was fascinated with the death of Yogi Paramahansa Yogananda, founder of the Self Realization Fellowship. Having read how Yogananda's body lay in an open casket at Forest Lawn for some twenty-one days without apparent decomposition, he hoped he too could achieve a similar state of consciousness.

Presley even enlisted the services of so-called spiritual advisor, hair-dresser, Larry Geller. One day Geller came upon Presley sitting in Graceland's Trophy Room - Bible in his lap - in tears. "Why are you cry-ing?" Geller asked.

"Because I'm not Jewish." Thereafter, Elvis always wore around his neck both a cross and Star of David. "I don't want to miss out on heaven because of a technicality!" he would joke.

On the Vegas stage Presley diligently honed his new act, which includ-ed choreography taken directly from the martial arts. By 1970 the Colonel was confident enough to send Presley out on the road once again. Beginning on 27th February with the first of six dates at the Houston Astrodome, Elvis would spend the rest of his life touring and giv-

An early design for the Elvis stamp.

ing well over one hundred performances a year, never playing to an empty seat.

One particular highlight came during a series of four concerts in June, 1972 at New York's Madison Square Garden, when Elvis pulled in $740,000 in ticket sales and broke all previous Garden records. The weekly magazine *Variety* said of the performance, "Presley was a backwoods phenomenon whose blues style and hip swivelling antics scandalized his elders. But now Presley is a highly polished, perfectly timed machine, a superstar."

Colonel Parker continued to do extremely well out of Presley's career. Elvis signed a new contract on 4th February, 1972, giving Parker one third of his tour earnings - a very high rate of commission by any standards. It seemed that the Colonel was in need of ready cash, having acquired a costly gambling habit. While Presley performed in the Showroom, Parker played in the casinos and, reportedly, was losing a million dollars a year to the Las Vegas Hilton alone.

Parker's associate, Jean Aberbach recalls, "He was the most wonderful human being God created, but once he came to Vegas I couldn't recognize him. Until that time the Colonel didn't even want to spend one dollar on anything; he used to hustle everybody, make them pay for everything. All of a sudden, this same person lost up to a million a year."

By 1973 Parker found himself with another difficulty. Offers were pouring in from overseas for Elvis to do a world tour. In Britain the offer was more than one million dollars plus travel on a private airliner. Japan promptly doubled the offer. Parker couldn't accompany Elvis overseas, however, because he himself had no passport. It seems that the Colonel may have been living in the USA unlawfully, and he feared that, if word got out, he would be deported immediately.

Once more, however, the crafty old hustler found a way out. If he couldn't send Elvis to the world then the world would come to Elvis. He got the idea from a recent Mohammed Ali fight that had been beamed all round the globe via satellite.

The ninety minute concert, 'Elvis Aloha From Hawaii', staged at Honolulu's International Arena on 14th January, 1973, was the ultimate spectacle. Resplendent in a white Bill Belew jumpsuit with hand-sewn gems, Presley essentially brought his Vegas act to a staggering one billion people, in forty countries. This was more than had watched the first moon landing by Apollo 11. Finishing the explosive performance by tossing his $8,000 cap into the audience, he had scored an undeniable coup. No entertainer had ever played to a larger audience.

"It was a performance not unlike Streisand's Central Park gathering that became a television milestone. But overall it was one of those rare TV moments, every inch the quality showcase for its star," hailed one impressed critic.

However, it was to be Presley's final triumph. Only days after the performance, Priscilla announced that she wanted out of their five year marriage. For years their relationship had slowly been breaking down. Presley was on the road for six months of the year and forbade his wife to join him or even to occupy her long, lonely hours with schooling or a job. When he was at home Graceland was invaded by the Memphis Mafia, along with their girlfriends, taking up residence in the mansion. There was no privacy in the Presley marriage.

Priscilla had matured and become much more perceptive, and was no longer prepared to tolerate Elvis' ever-increasing neurotic need for control. In the face of Presley's frequent and lengthy absences, she had forged a life of her own with dance and art classes, and even dared to offer constructive criticism of his work, despite once having a chair hurled at her in a display of the notorious Presley temper.

Elvis' and Priscilla's relationship had certainly suffered from an absence of sexual intimacy following the birth of Lisa Marie, which suggested an Oedipus complex of some sort. Priscilla later revealed, "He had mentioned before we were married that he had never been able to make love to a woman who'd had a child. I didn't understand at the time, but later I would learn about men who are very close to their own mothers. Elvis even told me the many nights when Gladys was ill he would sleep with her. He told me I was a young mother now, that being the mother of his child is very special. My physical and emotional needs were unfulfilled."

Priscilla, however, found comfort in the arms of her karate instructor, Mike Stone, and she left Elvis on 23rd February, 1972. A stunned Elvis accepted that the marriage was irrevocably broken, and the union was formally dissolved on 9th October, 1973, with Priscilla receiving a generous settlement, leaving her financially secure.

J.D. Sumner remembers a distraught Elvis calling him into his bedroom, lamenting, "Where did I go wrong? Priscilla is the only thing I ever wanted."

"I told him, 'You've heard that a woman's home is her castle? Well Elvis, Priscilla didn't have a home. She couldn't even come out of the bedroom unless she was fully clothed. You had thirty bodyguards standing around.'"

Earl Greenwood has a deeper analysis of the demise of the Presley marriage: "Desperate from the lack of control he felt over his life, Elvis viewed Priscilla not as a person but as a solution. He was losing his balance on the ledge over the abyss that yawned beneath him and he counted on her to grab on and not let him slip off. Priscilla did her best, but found it impossible to save Elvis from himself."

It was becoming clear that Presley had become his own worst enemy. The tragedy to come would provide terrible confirmation of this.

CHAPTER SIX

EXODUS

"I keep wondering, will this all last? And my heart gets to beating so fast I can't sleep. I have this recurring dream that everything's gone: the Colonel, the money, the fans at the gate, the girls. I dream that I'm all by myself."

Elvis Presley

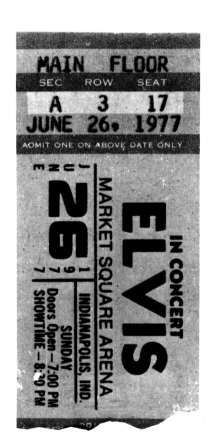

Above: The most coveted of all tickets - a good seat at an Elvis concert. This ticket is for the last concert which Elvis gave on 26th June, 1977.
Opposite: In Las Vegas towards the end.

IN THE FINAL INCARNATION OF ELVIS PRESLEY the Colonel's ultimate ideal was, at last, achieved. The image was that of a fairground sideshow, a glittery, gilded, gaudy Elvis decked out in gold tunics and sequinned capes, decorated with rings and chains, making his grand entrance to Strauss's *So Sprach Zarathustra* (the theme of *2001*) and crooning *My Way* and *It's Now Or Never* to audiences who'd shuffle off to Wayne Newton's show the next night.

By the mid seventies Presley, his bloated body coiled with Saranwrap to sweat off the fat, was an act who had descended into parody. Columnist James Wolcott of the *Village Voice* wrote, "Elvis is a figure whose significance shrinks with each passing season. As a musical artist he doesn't exist, he doesn't begin to exist."

Sadly, the years of excess had finally caught up with him: the endless series of self-seeking women, the steady diet of cheeseburgers and fried peanut butter sandwiches, and the punishing tour schedule that would have exhausted a man half his age. The once virile and athletic entertainer was now affected by chronic health problems including glaucoma, a twisted colon and recurring respiratory distress.

It was probably his increasing drug use, however, that contributed most to his deterioration. "From *GI Blues* on you can notice the way he speaks," reveals Red West. "He had to make a real effort to slow his speech down. He would talk like a machine gun in those movies where he was wired with uppers. He was high the whole time."

Presley's dependence became far more insidious. Dexies escalated to Desbutal, Valium to the heavy duty downer, Placidyl. Stated Red: "He takes pills to go to sleep. He takes pills to get up. He takes pills to go to the john and he takes pills to stop him going to the john. The pills do all

The Presleys leave the Santa Monica court-room following their amicable divorce on 10th October, 1973.

the work for him. He is a walking pharmaceutical shop."

Ironically, Presley abhorred street drugs, but thought nothing of consuming drugs prescribed by a number of doctors, including his personal physician, Dr. George Nichopoulos, dubbed 'Dr. Nick'. As Rick Stanley put it, "There were no doctors that said, 'No,' to Elvis. They all gave him whatever he wanted, anytime he wanted it."

Presley entertains ....

Vernon Presley, despite his often rocky relationship with his son, was the only person who made a concerted effort to rescue him from drug abuse. From 1969-1975 he hired private detectives to track down his son's drug sources. When confronted, however, Elvis threatened to cut off his $75,000 annual salary.

"It's my life and I'll do what I want with it!" he snapped at his father.

By 1975 Presley's heavy drug use had begun to affect his performance. He often forgot lyrics on stage and slurred his words. His temperament was affected as well. "Their breath smells like they have been eating catfish," was his insensitive introduction of his all-black back-up singers. When vocalist, Kathy Westmoreland, politely requested an alternative introduction to the jokey but somewhat insulting one Elvis liked to use, he humiliated her on stage: "This is Kathy Westmoreland, who doesn't like the way I introduce her...and if she doesn't like it she can get the hell off the stage!" In fact she and two members of the Sweet Inspirations walked off the stage in protest.

Another time country singer, Jimmy Dean, waited an hour to visit Presley in his dressing room. When Elvis finally showed, Dean said jokingly, "I'm out to rip a yard from your ass for keeping me waiting."

Presley pulled out his .22 revolver, stuck it under Dean's chin and

snarled, "And I ought to blow your head off for talking to me like that."

During the last two years of his life, death threats, lingering torment over the loss of Priscilla and declining health forced Elvis to lead a life of virtual seclusion. Hidden away at Graceland, he was also becoming preoccupied with death. "I don't feel I'll live a long life. I won't live to be fifty," he said repeatedly. His fascination with death led him to watch a mortician embalm a friend and also to take midnight excursions through graveyards with close members of his entourage.

Bodyguard Sonny West (cousin of Red) remembers: "The worst of all was his return to the funeral home where his mother was laid out. He would go through at three in the morning and wander around the slabs looking at all the embalmed bodies. We came into this big room with heads sticking from under sheets. They were bodies and they were sort of tilted upward, feet first. Then Elvis starts walking around lifting the sheets telling us all the cosmetic things morticians do when people are in accidents. It scared the shit out of me."

By 1976 Elvis had graduated to the most potent painkillers: the opium-based, class A narcotics Demerol and Dialudid, a drug even stronger than heroin. His entourage spoke of Presley's many overdoses, of reviving him with oxygen and of follow-up hospital stays for detoxification. Elvis' valet, James Caughley, relates that within the space of nine months, "We had three ODs; it was unbelievable. On this occasion in Vegas he had hardly any circulation in his body, hardly any heartbeat. Several of the boys set Elvis up in a chair. Nichopoulos had his bag with him."

One night Elvis was partying with a teenage girl the Memphis Mafia had picked up, and they both accidentally overdosed on Hycodan, an addictive cough medicine. While Presley came out of it relatively quickly, the girl lay unconscious for over twenty-four hours, until a desperate Elvis phoned the Colonel as she was carried out on a stretcher, close to death. Parker came to the rescue, keeping the incident out of the papers, paying off relatives and successfully preventing an official inquiry. Fortunately the girl recovered. On 29th May, 1977, Elvis walked off the stage during a concert in Baltimore - the first time he had ever stopped in the middle of a concert for health reasons.

On 21st June in Rapid City, South Dakota, on the final leg of his summer tour, Elvis was preparing for a television documentary, dressed in a yellow jumpsuit embellished with an Inca mosaic of jewels. Puffy, white-faced and blinking in the bright lights, he paused backstage and whispered to his stepbrother, "Know what Rick? I may not look too good for my television special tonight, but I'll look good in my coffin."

Five days later at the Market Square Arena in Indianapolis, he came off stage ready to collapse. It would be his final public appearance.

Less than two months later, at home in Graceland, on the evening of 15th August, 1977, Elvis went to the office of dentist, Lester Hoffman, to have a cavity filled. Plagued with his usual insomnia, Presley watched television until around 4.00 am. Then he engaged a few of the guys in a

Elvis' terrific smile burned into the memory of many faithful fans.

Opposite: Presley showing his famous double chins.

Right: With 'tricky Dicky' at the White House in the seventies.

Below: With long time aid, close friend and confidant, Joe Esposito.

game of racquetball until 6.00 am. According to Elvis' girl-friend, Ginger Alden, he was still having trouble sleeping and went into the bathroom to read. Ginger fell asleep and woke at 2.00 pm the next afternoon to discover Elvis slumped on the bathroom floor.

Paramedics, along with Dr. Nick, rushed to the scene and desperately worked on Presley. En route to the hospital, however, signs of rigor mortis were already appearing. At the age of forty-two, the king of rock'n'roll was dead.

As the news went out, radio stations all over the world interrupted their programming to play Elvis hits. President Jimmy Carter issued the following statement: "Elvis Presley's death deprives our country of a part of itself. His music and personality fusing the styles of white country and black rhythm and blues permanently changed the face of American popular culture. He was a symbol to people the world over of the vitality, rebelliousness and good humor of his country."

Within hours of the announcement, crowds of mourners gathered at Graceland's gates. Observed writer Martin Torgoff: "It was a densely packed human mass of sorrow and respect of every imaginable social,

Presley on his last holiday with girlfriend Ginger in Hawaii.

political, ethnic grouping and religious persuasion, a broad cross-section of the America that Elvis Presley had reached for and been able to put in his pocket, there because they were trying to clutch onto something that had also died in them that day."

The funeral, two days later, was attended by twenty heads of state and covered live by all the main television networks. Crowds packed the three-mile route from Graceland to Forest Lawn, some on rooftops, others perched in trees watching the motorcade of seventeen white limousines escort their idol to his grave. Colonel Parker declined to be a pallbearer, watching instead from a police motorcycle some distance away, while Dr. Nick was chosen to help carry the body to the Forest Lawn mausoleum along with Joe Esposito, Lamar Fitze (a prominent member of the Memphis Mafia), Charlie Hodge and Elvis' cousin, Billy Smith.

Rumours were rife about the cause of Presley's death. Although the official cause of death was given as cardiac arrest, claims of suicide, murder and even bone cancer appeared in the media. Extraordinary revelations came to light in a grand jury investigation of Dr. Nichopoulos. In the final twenty months of Elvis' life, Dr. Nick had apparently prescribed a staggering 12,000 amphetamines, sedatives and narcotics to the superstar, although he claimed that he believed that these were intended for Presley's entire entourage. Although he had his medical license sus-

Presley's very public funeral.

Opposite, main picture: Pallbearers carry Elvis' coffin to Forest Hills Cemeteries Mausoleum for his last rites.
Opposite, inset: Vernon Presley leaves a Memphis courtroom after the reading of Elvis' will on 22nd August, 1977.

pended for three months, he was cleared in court of malpractice and unethical conduct.

In a meticulous investigation, ABC news producer, Charles Thompson, came to a very different conclusion. Thompson contended that, following the visit to his dentist on the night of 15th August, Elvis mistakenly took ten therapeutic doses of the painkiller codeine, a drug to which he was severely allergic. Unable to tolerate the narcotic, he suffered a violent and fatal reaction. Thompson was convinced that the cause of death was actually an accidental overdose of multiple drugs.

Elvis' death was very bad news for Colonel Tom Parker. The courts ruled that Parker had no legal rights or interest to the Presley estate and he was forced to relinquish any connection to the Elvis Presley name. As a result, Parker sold his rights to some seven hundred Presley songs and relinquished all "rights, titles and interest" in all Presley related contracts for a paltry sum of two million dollars.

The Colonel, without his high level business connections, was evicted from his suite at the Las Vegas Hilton and retired to Palm Springs.

Almost two decades after his death, Elvis Presley's mystique lives on. Each year on the anniversary of his death thousands of loyal pilgrims flock to Graceland to join in the candlelight vigil held in the Meditation Garden, where Elvis is buried alongside his parents and grandmother.

Today Elvis Presley is still big business, with total record sales revenues

Vernon paying his respects at his son's grave.

now in excess of one billion dollars, and Elvis memorabilia a booming multi-million dollar annual enterprise. Professional impersonators everywhere are cashing in on the Presley persona, and tabloids around the world carry stories of countless Elvis 'sightings'.

One stalwart follower summed up the Presley fascination like this: "We're the Elvis generation. Waxed fruit on our kitchen table, brand X in our cabinets, a mortgage on our home and a love in our hearts that cannot be explained or rained out. He was one of us...the believers in

4E   77

ELVIS ARON PRESLEY

Elvis Presley was born in Tupelo, Mississippi on January 8, 1935, the son of Vernon and Gladys Presley. He moved to Memphis in 1948. Soon after signing a contract with Sun Records in 1954 he achieved tremendous popularity. His musical and acting career in records, movies, television, and concerts made him one of the most successful and outstanding entertainers in the world. He died on August 16, 1977 and is buried here at his Memphis home, Graceland.

TENNESSEE   HISTORICAL   COMMISSION

The historic plaque outside Graceland.

magic and fairytales."

Southern novelist William Price Fox put it another way: "He wasn't like anyone. You start trying to compare Elvis to something and you can forget it. All you can do with a talent that big and that different is sort of point at it when you see it going by, and maybe listen for the ricochet."

To millions around the globe, Elvis Aron Presley was and is more than a mere popular entertainer. He was bigger than life, even bigger, ultimately, than death. He was quite simply, the King.

Acknowledgements

Senior Editors: Brenda Giuliano and Sara Colledge
Executive Researcher: Sesa Nichole Giuliano
Intern: Devin Giuliano

The authors would like to thank the following people for their kindness in helping to publish this book.

Sriman Jagannatha Dasa Adikari
Dr. Mirza Beg
Stefano Castino
Srimati Vrinda Rani Devi Dasi
Enzo of Valentino
Robin Scot Giuliano
Avalon and India Giuliano
ISKCON
Tim Hailstone
Suneel Jaitly

Jo Messham
Marcus Lecky
His Divine Grace B.H. Mangalniloy Goswami Maharaja
Dr. Michael Klapper
Donald Lehr
Timothy Leary
Andrew Lownie
Mark Studios, Clarence, New York
David Lloyd McIntyre
His Divine Grace A.C. Bhaktivedanta Swami Prabhupada
Self Realization Institute of America (SRI)
Sean Smith

Wendell and Joan Smith
Something Fishy Productions Ltd.
Dave Thompson
Edward Veltman
Dr. Ronald Zucker

Photo credits

The Official Elvis Presley Fan Club of Great Britain: title page, 6, 7, 8, 10, 11, 14, 16, 17, 18, 19 (top), 20, 22, 23, 24, 25, 26, 27, 28, 29, 30, 31, 33, 34, 35, 37, 39, 40, 41, 42 (left), 43, 44, 45, 48, 49, 50, 53, 55, 57, 58, 59 (below), 61, 66, 70, 73, 74.

Square Circle Archives: half title page, 13, 19 (below), 21, 32, 36, 38, 42 (right), 46, 47, 51, 52, 56, 59 (top), 60, 62, 63, 65, 69, 71, 72, 75, 76, 77, 78, 79, 80, 81, 82, 84, 85, 86, 87, 88, 89, 90, 91, 92, 93, 94, 95, 96.